Travel Adventures

# Tulum
## National Park

Addition

**Logan Avery**

## Consultants

**Colene Van Brunt**
Math Coach
Hillsborough County Public Schools

## Publishing Credits

Rachelle Cracchiolo, M.S.Ed., *Publisher*
Conni Medina, M.A.Ed., *Managing Editor*
Dona Herweck Rice, *Series Developer*
Emily R. Smith, M.A.Ed., *Series Developer*
Diana Kenney, M.A.Ed., NBCT, *Content Director*
June Kikuchi, *Content Director*
Susan Daddis, M.A.Ed., *Editor*
Karen Malaska, M.Ed., *Editor*
Kevin Panter, *Senior Graphic Designer*

**Image Credits:** p.12 National Geographic Creative/Bridgeman Images; p.13 Javi Az/
Shutterstock; p.15 Pictures From History/Newscom; p.16 Nido Huebl/Shutterstock; p.18
Patryk Kosmider/Shutterstock; all other images from iStock and/or Shutterstock.

**Library of Congress Cataloging-in-Publication Data**

Names: Avery, Logan, author.
Title: Travel adventures : Tulum National Park / Logan Avery.
Other titles: Tulum National Park
Description: Huntington Beach, CA : Teacher Created Materials, [2019] |
Summary: "Visiting Tulum National Park is like going back in time. The
Maya lived there long ago. Add as you explore the things they left
behind"-- Provided by publisher. | Includes index. | Audience: K to 3 |
Identiers: LCCN 2017054974 (print) | LCCN 2018030005 (ebook) | ISBN
9781480759800 (eBook) | ISBN 9781425856861 | ISBN 9781425856861?q(pbk.)
Subjects: LCSH: Tulum Site (Mexico)--Guidebooks--Juvenile literature. |
Mayas--Antiquities--Guidebooks--Juvenile literature. | Tulum Site
(Mexico)--Guidebooks. sears | Mayas--Guidebooks. sears | LCGFT: Guidebooks.
Classi cation: LCC F1435.1.T8 (ebook) | LCC F1435.1.T8 A94 2019 (print) |
DDC 972/.01--dc23
LC record available at https://lccn.loc.gov/2017054974

## Teacher Created Materials

5301 Oceanus Drive
Huntington Beach, CA 92649-1030
www.tcmpub.com

**ISBN 978-1-4258-5686-1**

# Table of Contents

# An Old Place

The world is old. People have lived here for a long time. They have built homes and other buildings.

These are some of the ruins in Tulum.

A few of the oldest places still **exist**. One of those places is Tulum (too-LOOM). It has many **ruins**.

Tulum is on the **coast** of Mexico. It was one of the first cities built with a wall around it. Now, it is a national park.

This temple is the largest building in Tulum.

Mexico

**LET'S DO MATH!**

Barry walks 30 steps to a ruin. He walks 50 more steps to the beach. How many total steps does Barry walk? Solve using groups of ten.

# Visiting Tulum

People from around the world visit Tulum. They come to see the ruins. They come to see the land and beaches, too.

Tulum is known for its beauty. The green land touches the rocky **cliffs**. The cliffs drop down to the sandy beach. Blue water flows in and out along the **shore**.

A class takes a trip to Tulum. Mr. Brook brings 32 students. Miss Sanchez brings 7 students. How many students are there now? Draw or place objects on a place value chart to solve. Write an equation to show your thinking.

| Tens | Ones |
|------|------|
|      |      |

# The Ruins

The Maya built the city of Tulum. They lived there long ago. They were safe there for many years.

Maya boats bring goods to Tulum.

Later, people came from Spain. They took over the land. They destroyed the Maya.

These statues show the Spanish people taking over the Maya.

Buildings were important to the Maya. They built many of them.

The ruins at Tulum were palaces and **pyramids**. They are **worn** now. But you can tell what they used to look like.

Maya people work at the large temple.

Many pools are near the ruins.  They are sunken holes in the land.  The holes are filled with water.

The Maya used the pools. People visit the pools today when they go to Tulum.

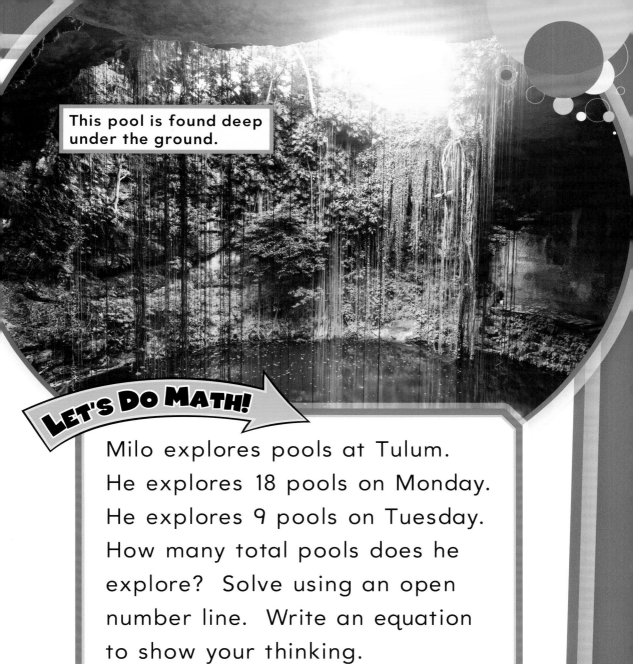

This pool is found deep under the ground.

## LET'S DO MATH!

Milo explores pools at Tulum. He explores 18 pools on Monday. He explores 9 pools on Tuesday. How many total pools does he explore? Solve using an open number line. Write an equation to show your thinking.

⟵————————————⟶

# Old and New

Tulum National Park is busy. Many people go there. They go to see the beauty. They also go to see how things used to be.

The old world and the new world are both found at Tulum.

These dancers perform while dressed as Maya.

# ⚙ Problem Solving

Laurel takes photos on her visit to Tulum. Use the table to answer the questions. Show your thinking using words, numbers, or pictures.

1.  How many photos of ruins and pools does Laurel take?

2.  How many photos of ruins and beaches does Laurel take?

3.  Laurel wants to take 100 total photos. How many more photos will she take?

| Places | Number of Photos |
| --- | --- |
| ruins | 43 |
| beaches | 20 |
| pools | 30 |

# Glossary

**cliffs**—steep areas of land that drop straight down

**coast**—the land near the edge of a body of water

**exist**—to be real

**pyramids**—large buildings with square-shaped bases and triangle-shaped faces

**ruins**—old buildings that have broken down over time

**shore**—the land near the edge of a body of water

**worn**—broken down

# Index

# Answer Key

## Let's Do Math!

**page 7:**

80 steps

**page 11:**

Charts should show
3 tens and 9 ones;
32 + 7 = 39

**page 17:**

27 pools;

18 + 9 = 27

## Problem Solving

**1.** 73 photos

**2.** 63 photos

**3.** 7 photos